KUMI
NEW-GENERATION AFRICAN POETS
A CHAPBOOK BOX SET

INTRODUCTION BY
KWAME DAWES & CHRIS ABANI

No part of this book may be reproduced, stored in a retrieval system, or transmitted in any form, by any means, including mechanical, electronic, photocopying, recording, or otherwise, without the prior written consent of the publisher.

Published by Akashic Books
©2024 Kwame Dawes and Chris Abani

ISBN for full box set: 978-1-63614-188-6
Library of Congress Control Number for full box set: 2024936282

All rights reserved
Printed in China
First printing

Akashic Books
Brooklyn, New York
Instagram, X, Facebook: AkashicBooks
info@akashicbooks.com
www.akashicbooks.com

African Poetry Book Fund
Prairie Schooner
University of Nebraska
110 Andrews Hall
Lincoln, Nebraska 68588

For Lorna,
Sena, Kekeli, Akua,
Mama the Great,
and the tribe: Gwyneth, Kojo, Adjoa, and Kojovi.
Remembering Aba and Neville.
K.D.

*

Remembering Daphne, Michael, and Greg;
and for Mark, Charles, and Stella—my family.
I love you.
C.A.

AFRICAN POETRY BOOK SERIES

SERIES EDITOR

Kwame Dawes

EDITORIAL BOARD

Chris Abani, Northwestern University
Gabeba Baderoon, Pennsylvania State University
Kwame Dawes, University of Nebraska–Lincoln
Phillippa Yaa de Villiers, University of the Witwatersrand
Bernardine Evaristo, Brunel University
Aracelis Girmay, Stanford University
John Keene, Rutgers University
Matthew Shenoda, Brown University

ADVISORY BOARD

Laura Sillerman
Glenna Luschei
Elizabeth Alexander
Sulaiman Adebowale

TISA: NEW-GENERATION AFRICAN POETS

Introduction by Kwame Dawes and Chris Abani

CONTENTS OF BOX SET

Crying in My Mother's Tongue
Qhali

A Failed Attempt at Undoing Memories
Dare Tunmise

Home Is a Heart That Flees
Nurain Ọládèjì

If the Golden Hour Won't Come for Us
Adams Adeosun

In These Bones, I Am Shifting
Claudia Owusu

I Watch You Disappear
Feranmi Ariyo

Light Through Water
Connor Cogill

Voyaging
Nome Emeka Patrick

Yaanom
Sarpong Osei Asamoah

KUMI: NEW-GENERATION AFRICAN POETS
Introduction
by Kwame Dawes and Chris Abani

I.

The singular lesson I have learned in the nearly ten years of editing these box sets and other projects for the African Poetry Book Fund is quite simple—gratitude. Gratitude is at the very core of Igbo and Yoruba worldviews. When you ask someone how they are in a casual greeting, they often reply: "I remain grateful." For me, gratitude is a practical matter and is, in this case, linked to foundations, community, and witness.

There is the remarkable foundation of the APBF—from the planning, vision, and ethics that went into its inception, the earlier models it was built on, and the serendipitous meeting of capital and potential, to the deep generosity of financial, publishing, and editorial partnerships. There are many reasons why APBF should not exist, but it does, and it continues to thrive and flourish. Gratitude.

The community that this convergence has generated is amazing: there is the volunteer-run editorial board comprising some of the most awarded and respected African poets of our time; the volunteer staff who support the work, many of them poets on the cusp of breaking out in their own careers; and the poets themselves, who have gone on to publish full-length books, to flourish in graduate programs, to support emerging poets and each other, and to steer others to this unique home we have built. Gratitude.

To continue to be able to edit and offer these books. To witness a thriving and flourishing aesthetic emergence in poetry—perhaps the largest and most diverse by nation, border, and identity—arising from the continent and its diaspora to date. To witness an explosion of work that will continue to grow and flourish long after Kwame and I hand over the project to the next generation. Gratitude.

Not all of these poets have MFAs or workshop experience; several of them emerged through community efforts and self-education. Yet these voices are nonetheless assured and mature. Often referring to other chapbooks in the series, these writers learn from *each other*. This is something we have seen evolve in intertextuality, conversations across crafts, subject matter, and even political concerns—we also see these as conversations on how to make poetry.

Adams Adeosun's chapbook *If the Golden Hour Won't Come for Us* begins with these lines:

> And above all, I desire cleanness,
>   baptism more than a scrubbing down,
>
> an animal softer than my body

It's a bold invitation to reclamation. It's prayer in its best form, a sort of blasphemy, and a negotiation with forces larger than oneself. In a way, it embodies the heart of the reggae aesthetic, which is simultaneously lamentation, social justice demand, and the sensuality of life. A form of gratitude, nonetheless.

In his chapbook *Light Through Water,* Cape Town poet Connor Cogill writes:

> This home has been
> in our family for generations. I will not ask
> whose war. I will not ask whose land. I will
> tell a charming story: how I was born
> ("Continent without a name")

Here we are invited into a self-implicating conversation about race within Africa—something not often addressed in conquest and colonialism—and a generation made collateral, both on the terms of the colonized and the colonizer.

Feranmi Ariyo's *I Watch You Disappear* offers ritual and internment of smoke in "The Last Smoke." He writes: "And once, after we learn he is never going to recover, / my soon-to-be-dead father asks for a cigarette." There is this constant attendance to the personal, the political, the communal—an engagement wrestling with the shapes, challenges, and pressures of being human. There are attempted negotiations with guilt, with lineage, with culpability, and much more. A true representation of the fact of one of my claims, which is that African writers are the curators of Africa's humanity.

Claudia Owusu's chapbook *In These Bones, I Am Shifting* explores the relationship of the body to shame, sacrifice, and complicity, though one belied by a collective hope. In these we find again the power of transformation, transubstantiation even, or one can say, a restatement of reclamation. Here water, which has been undergirding all the books in this box set, reveals the power to transform. In "Drown or Drought" she writes:

> In Taifa, my pee-stained bed sheets hung out on the line for the world to see.
> My cousins, siblings, and I spent the school break waiting for rain

I find myself unintentionally following water in this box set, as lineage, as ablution, as hope, as an uncompromising restitution, and as a thread. As editors we don't assign themes for the box sets, and we don't frame the call in this way either. But somehow, a dominant theme emerges, as though a collective unconscious has been formed. Gratitude.

In the chapbook *Crying in My Mother's Tongue*, South African poet Qhali writes:

> i found it above me on a tree and asked it why They didn't take me when i went in
> it got up and flew away   i followed it   umama told the psychiatrist
> ("the water returns to you")

This echoes the great Bessie Head, another South African writer, who struggled with a similar legacy. We see this most starkly in Head's *A Question of Power*, where she writes a kind of terrifying love, a kind of brokenness that is a more whole than wholeness and attempts to negotiate with the legacies of the trauma of apartheid and the continent's oppression. This impossible math, which is a kind of hope, runs through these chapbooks:

> Before the consecration,
> I was a light lost in my mother's womb
> —"Inheritance"
> *A Failed Attempt at Undoing Memories* by Dare Tunmise

Or when Nome Emeka Patrick writes in the poem "A Midnight Storm, Outside the Wild" from the chapbook *Voyaging*:

> The night is a wet grave. I'm in a room whose dark has eyes.

In the hands of less mature writers, these themes and subthemes, couched in such language, would be sentimental or disturbing. In the hands of these writers, they are disruptive but redemptive too.

Sarpong Osei Asamoah in *Yaanom* and the poem "Testimony" continues the thread unspooling throughout all these chapbooks:

> In my mother's garden, there's a bioluminescent wound in the
>   loam
> through which God spies on the world.
> I am the door.

And to bring the journey to an end, but also to restart it—here is Nurain Ọládèjì in "Facing East," a poem from his chapbook *Home is a Heart That Flees*:

> I turn to face east; everywhere else leads away
> from truth. I know because I followed each road

Follow the road, the thread, and the flow of water and words to the end of this offering and experience gratitude with me.

—Chris Abani

II.

> "Modernity is not always the answer, sometimes antiquity is, too."
> —*The Crown*

> "Elegies are one of the few places where we can do the work of care, not just to ourselves but to our dead . . ."
> —Romeo Oriogun

When we began this box set series, Chris Abani and I agreed to produce a set every year and that upon completing the tenth we would review the series and see what the steady and consistent gathering of new African voices in poetry offered. I believe we made a prudent decision, born of our circumstances, to refrain from dictating a direction for the poetry that we would solicit. Fully aware that despite our intentions, the fact that we were making our decisions around a set of values based on what we felt was poetry with vision, clarity, coherent and consistent ambition, and venturesomeness, each box set would send a message to emerging poets that could seem didactic.

Rather than proceed to shape a poetics for the series, we decided to suppress this instinct and replace it with consideration for the collective weight of the sixty to seventy manuscripts that came to us from all around the continent and her diaspora, as evidence of the state of poetry on the continent. We sought to be guided by what we were seeing, to test it all, and report on what we had seen. Abani's introduction to this box set is a brilliant, generous, and aptly exciting reporting of what we have seen and witnessed in these manuscripts. Abani has shown us that one of the most promising qualities emerging in these ten years of chapbooks, totaling more than a hundred poets, is the simple but meaningful fact that these poets are in conversation. They are reading each other because they have access to each other's writing. They are forming distinctive poetic visions, finding the points of connection between themselves as poets and their necessary differences. In some cases, these poets may know each other, but for the most part, they are meeting each other through their poems.

In many ways, these writers, consciously or unconsciously feeding each other, are pushing against a recent critique of contemporary African poetry that worried the work is imitative and derivative of non-African poetry. Superficially, there is evidence to support this claim. Phrases like "exit wounds" and titles that declare the poems as "self-portraits," as well as an inordinate number of "erasure" poems, "duplexes," and contrapuntal poems appear with faddish regularity. Yet in the best work, these are often borrowed suits trying and failing to contain the bodies of the poems emerging. Of course, there is no sin in this kind of imitation and dialogue. Rather than lament the influence of the West on African poetry, it is becoming increasingly clear that African poets are bringing new obsessions and preoccupations to poetry.

Put another way, the years of relative silence of African poets in print, not only on the world stage but in African countries across generations, has meant that poets writing today have a double gift: the exciting prospect of being chroniclers of their moment in a rapidly transforming world, and the feeling that they are serving as the first correspondents of their world, their landscape, and their particular cultural space. It is easy and wrong to overstate this role. For though it is factual to say that the publication of African poetry has been in the doldrums for many years, it is equally factual to say that African poetry in all its remarkable manifestations has never waned, but has thrived—as a powerful fact of the life of Africans in song, griot speak, proverbs, Indigenous poetic cycles, and ubiquitous performances throughout African cultures.

We have seen a splendid proliferation of African poetry in print doing the hard and necessary work of chronicling the sentiment of our time. Abani has made the phrase "a living archive" a central source of purpose and intentionality for this series and the other publishing ventures we have undertaken in African poetry. It is this that allows us to accept some of the limitations of our series. As many have discovered, our print runs are modest and some editions can now safely be called collectors' items. We are also aware that our distribution in Africa is limited by circumstances we can't control, though we are making great efforts to improve this. But we take comfort in the fact that these poets are in print, accessible, and creating a body of work. Our last edition, *TISA*, has been especially successful, featured on multiple best-of lists.

This is our tenth edition of the *New-Generation African Poets* series, and we remain committed to our partnership with Akashic Books and our friends and informal advisors around the world who send us recommendations of African poets to whom we ought to pay attention. This edition, as Abani eloquently points out, is a stunning body of truly exciting contemporary African poetry. Varied, accomplished, eclectic, wholly alive, and wonderfully revelatory of how younger African poets are writing nations and selves in these times.

In this gathering, there is a refreshing sense of the immediate and the future, but, and for me more critically, there is also a growing engagement with the past, with antiquity and tradition, with the bold and healing acknowledgment of the value of our past as Africans, of our ancestors and the legacy of this continent's power and beauty, qualities that have been threatened often by the ugliness of colonialism and imperialism.

We can say with great confidence that the present and future of African poetry is in very good hands.

—*Kwame Dawes*

KWAME DAWES is the author of numerous books of poetry and other works of fiction, criticism, and essays. His most recent poetry collection, *Sturge Town*, which was published by Peepal Tree Press in the UK and W. W. Norton in the US. Dawes is a George W. Holmes University Professor of English and Glenna Luschei Editor of *Prairie Schooner*. He teaches in the Pacific MFA Program and is the series editor of the African Poetry Book Series, director of the African Poetry Book Fund, and artistic director of the Calabash International Literary Festival. He is a Chancellor for the Academy of American Poets and a Fellow of the Royal Society of Literature. Dawes is the winner of the prestigious Windham/Campbell Award for Poetry and was a finalist for the 2022 Neustadt International Prize for Literature. In 2022, Kwame Dawes was awarded the Order of Distinction Commander class by the Government of Jamaica, and in 2024, he was appointed Poet Laureate of Jamaica.

CHRIS ABANI's prose includes *The Secret History of Las Vegas*, *Song for Night*, *The Virgin of Flames*, *Becoming Abigail*, *GraceLand*, and *Masters of the Board*. His poetry collections include *Smoking the Bible*, *Sanctificum*, *There Are No Names for Red*, *Feed Me the Sun*, *Hands Washing Water*, *Dog Woman*, *Daphne's Lot*, and *Kalakuta Republic*. He holds a BA and MA in English, an MA in gender and culture, and a PhD in literature and creative writing. Abani is the recipient of a PEN USA Freedom to Write Award, a Prince Claus Award, a Lannan Literary fellowship, a California Book Award, a Hurston/Wright Legacy Award, a PEN Beyond Margins Award, a PEN/Hemingway Award, and a Guggenheim fellowship. He won the prestigious 2024 UNT Rilke Prize and was a finalist for the 2024 Neustadt International Prize for Literature. He is also a member of the American Academy of Arts and Sciences. Born in Nigeria, he is currently on the board of trustees, a professor of English, and director of African Studies at Northwestern University.

Kokeb Zeleke is a multimedia artist from Ethiopia, Eritrea, Los Angeles, and the Bay Area in California. Her work seeks to reframe, sometimes quite literally, Black beauty and Black multiplicity through art and a social justice lens. Her notable mural, *the roads we've been*, has been transmuted through music and performance art by Spleen. Kokeb is often inspired by poetry and will paint in response to a collection of poems, or a body of work. Several of her paintings have been featured on book covers of such poetry books, and bodies of work and has exhibited her work internationally. She lives in the Bay Area with her family and houseplants. Learn more at: kokebart.com.